Moose

We're Asleep Dad

Simon Key is an author, dad, Twitter genius and the co-owner of the Big Green Bookshop in Wood Green, north London.

Moose Allain is an artist, cartoonist and prolific tweeter. He lives and works in Devon.

We're Asleep Dad

by
Simon Key

Illustrations
by Moose Allain

ΛNIMΛ

an imprint of Head of Zeus

First published in the UK by Anima,
an imprint of Head of Zeus Ltd, in 2017

Text copyright © Simon Key, 2017
Illustrations copyright © Moose Allain, 2017

9 7 5 3 1 2 4 6 8

A catalogue record for this book is available
from the British Library.

ISBN (HB): 9781786699343
ISBN (E): 9781786699336

Layout by Adrian McLaughlin

Printed and bound in Great Britain by
CPI Group (UK) Ltd, Croydon CR0 4YY

Head of Zeus Ltd
First Floor East
5–8 Hardwick Street
London EC1R 4RG
WWW.HEADOFZEUS.COM

contents

introduction

I wake up at 5.12 am. That's when a small bundle of nonsense and joy bursts into our bedroom and throws himself onto our bed.

"Can I have some water?"

I stagger out of bed and head downstairs to find a cup to fill.

When I get back upstairs, we have more questions to answer.

"Can I have a dog?"

"Not right now."

"WHY…?"

"Well, it's half past five in the morning."

My daughter bursts into our room…

"HELLO!!" She bellows as she piles onto our bed.

"It's very early… Any chance you can try and sleep for a bit longer?"

"Dad… Mum… I have a question…"

"Yes… What is it?"

"Can you fly?"

"Um, no…"

"Can unicorns fly?"

"I guess they can, yes."

"Can I have some water?"

"OK, let's all go downstairs."

And so begins another day. Negotiations over breakfast, brushing teeth and getting ready for school will undoubtedly follow over the next three hours as the kids check out new videos on YouTube and build a new fortress on Minecraft.

I will be labelled a doofnugget for putting the cereal in the wrong bowl and Mum will be enrolled to put my daughter's hair into an acceptable plait.

It's exhausting, but I wouldn't have it any other way.

Our kids lighten up our lives with their enthusiasm, fun and seemingly endless curiosity. Even when we're desperately trying to get them to sleep or persuading them to do their homework for the umpteenth time, they'll say or do something that warms our hearts.

This book started as a series of tweets I used to do each night after I'd "tried" to get my kids to go to sleep. It seemed to resonate with a lot of people and the idea grew. It was a relief to be reminded that I wasn't the only one who was experiencing this nightly battle of wits. And more importantly, it was a reminder that they're just kids and all they want to do is to have fun. I can't emphasise this point strongly enough and I hope that most of the time at least, my kids' lives are full of the happiness and fun they deserve.

This book is for them.

Bedtime

My kids are asleep. I know this because I can hear that pretend snoring that kids do coming from their room.

My kids are asleep. I know this because when I saw them in the kitchen just now, they told me they were sleepwalking.

My kids are asleep. I know this because they've just woken me up to tell me.

My kids are asleep. I know this because two of their soft toys just poked their heads around the door and told me.

My kids are asleep. I know this because an aeroplane with a "hey Dad, we're asleep" banner has just flown past my flat.

My kids are asleep. I know this because they've just asked me to "tell Mum we're asleep."

13

My kids are asleep. I know this because I just got this telegram. "HELLO DADDY, STOP. WE ARE DEFINITELY ASLEEP. STOP. FROM YOUR KIDS. STOP."

My kids are asleep. I know this because they've just posted an Instagram picture of themselves with their eyes closed.

My kids are asleep. I know this because Donald Trump has tweeted that they are awake.

Dad's asleep. We know this because we just found him slumped in front of the computer. We'll get him to bed now. Love, the kids.

My kids are asleep. I know this because they've just updated their Facebook status to "asleep".

My kids are asleep. I know this even though I can hear them jumping up & down on their beds.

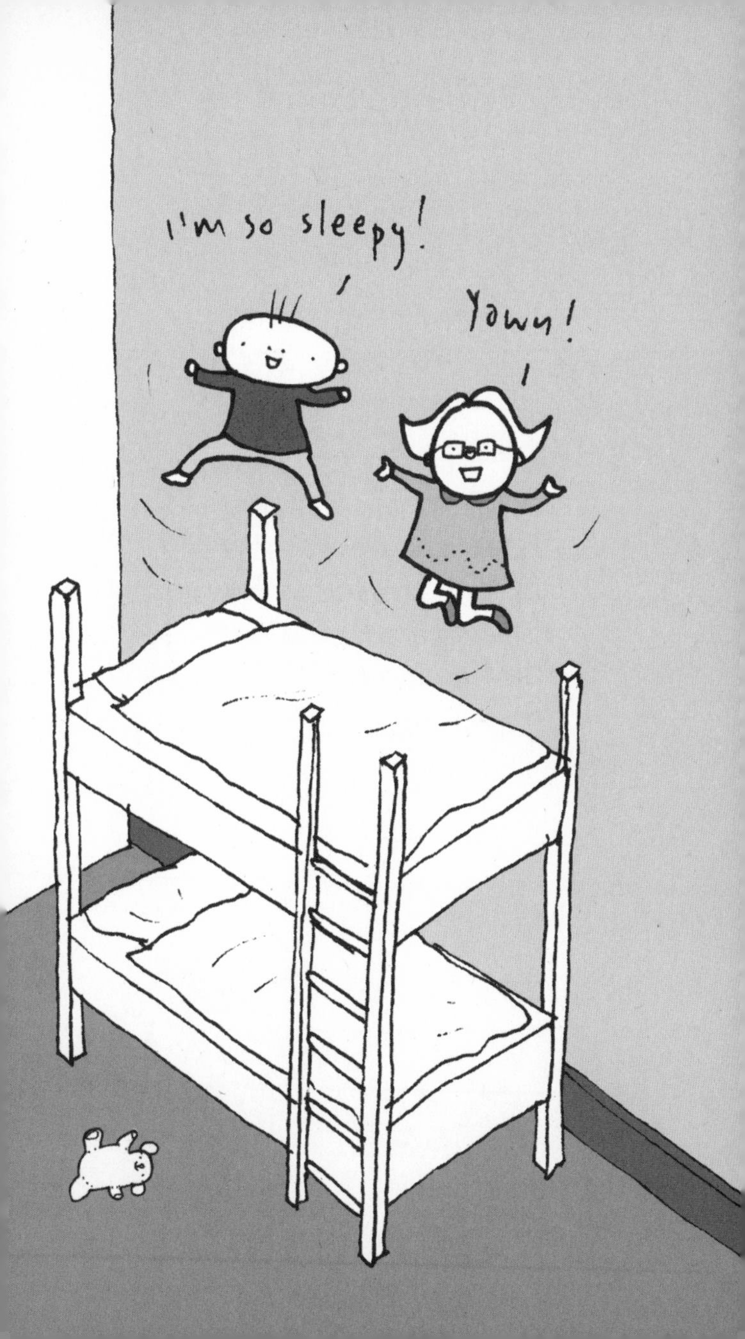
I'm so sleepy!
Yawn!

My kids are asleep. I know this because a pizza delivery guy just turned up with a thin crust margherita for "the kids asleep upstairs".

My kids are asleep. I know this because... Oh let's be honest. Of course they're not asleep.

My kids are asleep. I know this because they've been singing their new song "We're asleep Dad" non-stop for the last 35 minutes.

School

My kids have done their homework. I know this because they have hidden every pen & pencil in the house.

My kids love school. I know this because their new song "School is Rubbish" is the highest new entry in the Official Singles Chart.

My kids are ready to go to school. I know this because they're sitting in their pyjamas and I've just found their school uniforms stuffed under their mattresses.

My kids love school. I know this because their YouGov petition calling for a five day weekend is currently being discussed in the House of Commons.

My kids enjoyed school. I know this even though the headteacher has asked them not to sell "Down With Homework" badges and t-shirts during break time.

My kids have done their homework. I know this because according to them this week their homework was to play 3 hours of **MINECRAFT**.

My kids enjoyed school today.
I know this because they've
just handed me a letter.
"To Dad, School is closed tomorrow,
love from our teachers."

My kids have done their homework. I know this because when I told them to do it they both fell fast asleep.

My kids enjoyed school today. I know this because when I went to pick them up I found they had organised a 200-strong protest in the playground demanding their release.

My kids have done their homework. I know this because when I asked them they ran upstairs & barricaded themselves in their bedroom.

My kids are doing their homework. I know this because "can I have a snack", "I need the toilet", "can I have some water", "I have a hurty foot", "I'm tired", "I need the toilet too."

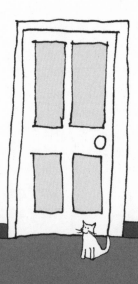

My kids enjoy school. I know this because they've presented me with their 'birth certificates' which show they are 18 & no longer need to go.

Just dropped my kids off at school. I know this because they just overtook me on their scooters as I was walking home.

My kids enjoyed school today. I know this because a teacher discovered plans for a tunnel they were going to dig entitled "escape route c."

My kids are doing their homework. I know this because I just heard one of them ask the other what level they were on and I can't find their iPad.

My kids enjoyed school today.
I know this because when I went
to pick them up, they charged
out of the classroom screaming
"SAVE US!!!"

My kids have done their homework. I know this even though the hamster has used their homework books as bedding.

My kids have done their homework.
I know this although for the fourth week in a row their teacher lost their homework books.

Going Out

My kids are ready to go out. I know this because they've hidden all their clothes.

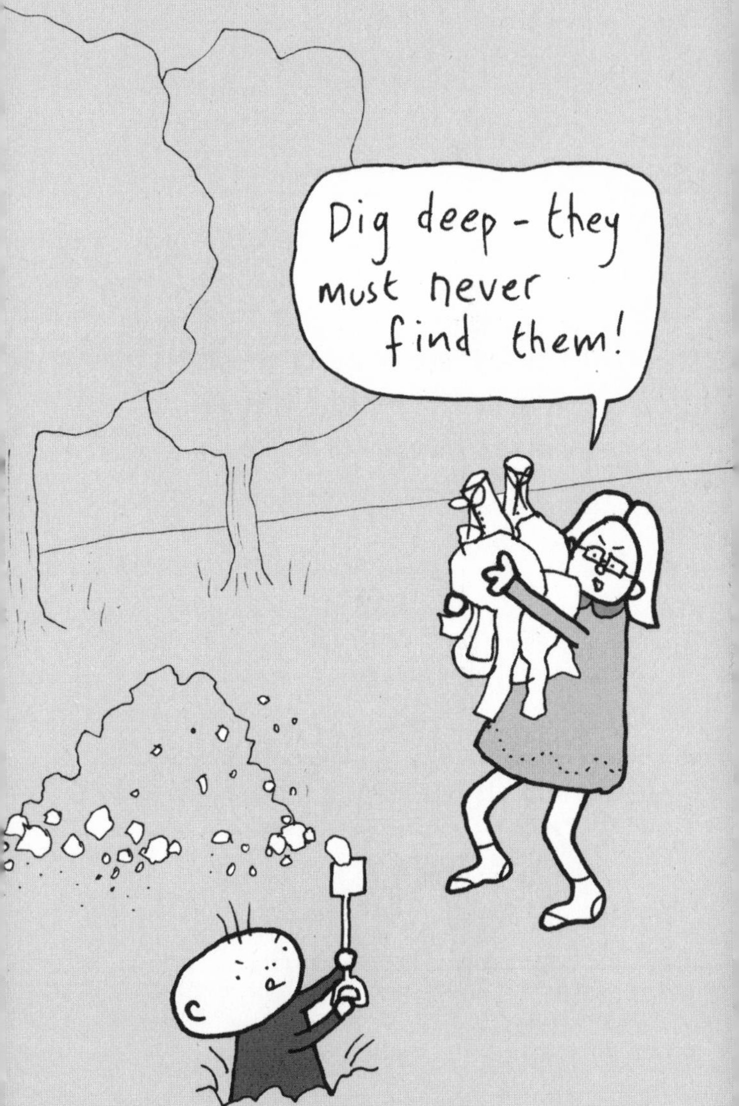
Dig deep - they must never find them!

My kids are enjoying our day out together. I know this because they've just phoned for a taxi to take them home.

My kids enjoyed their day out in the country today. I know this because they reprogrammed the Sat Nav and we ended up at the local toyshop.

My kids are ready to go out. I know this because I've asked them 5 times & they haven't moved from the sofa.

My kids are ready to go out.
I know this because they put
their clothes on inside out
because "it's funny."

My kids are ready to go out. I know this because they now want to perform a circus show for me in the front room.

My kids are ready to go out. I know this because they've just told me their tablet has 2% battery left & needs charging.

My kids are enjoying our walk in the woods. I know this because they've just thrown their wellies into a tree.

My kids are ready to go out. I know this because they want me to play their new game "find the door key."

My kids are off to a party. I know this because they want to keep the present we bought & are refusing to write in the card.

My kids are enjoying our trip to the supermarket. I know this because they've replaced all the food in the trolley with **MINECRAFT** minifigures.

My kids are ready to go out. I know this because it's pouring with rain & apparently they left their coats at school yesterday.

My kids are looking forward to going out. I know this because they've just handed me a doctor's note signing them off from going out for the rest of the day.

My kids enjoyed our family day out. I know this because I counted how many times they said they wanted to go home and it was 76. A new record.

My kids are ready to go out. I know this because one has handed me a note saying "I will tell you where my brother is if you give me £50".

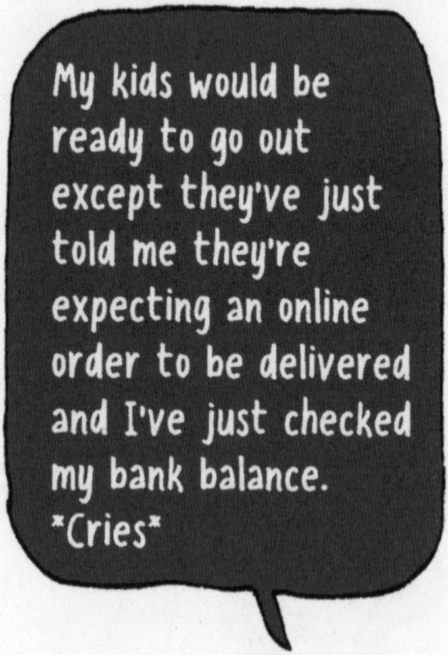
My kids would be ready to go out except they've just told me they're expecting an online order to be delivered and I've just checked my bank balance. *Cries*

Mealtimes

My kids enjoyed dinner. I know this because a carrot has just hit me on the back of my head.

My kids enjoyed dinner. I know this because they've just enrolled me into a 'basic cookery' class at our local night school.

My kids enjoyed dinner. I know this because I just found all the food under the dining table.

My kids enjoyed dinner. I know this because they are chanting "Yuck, yuck, yuck."

My kids enjoyed dinner. I know this because they've just set up a Crowdfunder to raise money for a takeaway pizza.

My kids enjoyed dinner. I know this because they've just registered the domain name www.dadcannotcook.com

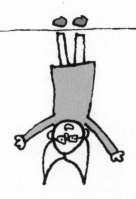

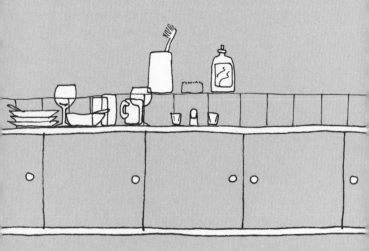

My kids enjoyed dinner. I know this because they just asked me what is the most effective way of getting rid of a horrible taste in the mouth.

My kids enjoyed dinner. I know this because when I just put my shoes on, one was full of pasta.

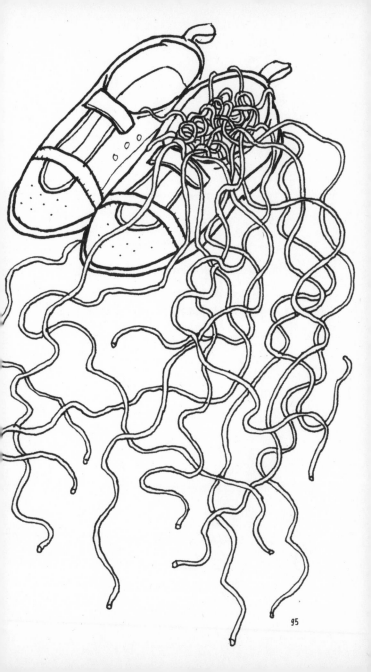

My kids enjoyed breakfast. I know this because they have told me they're now too ill to go to school.

My kids enjoyed dinner. I know this even though all of it 'fell' off their plates.

My kids are enjoying lunch. I know this because they've arranged the peas on their plates to spell 'BAD' & 'YUCK'.

My kids enjoyed dinner. I know this because they asked me which cookbook I got the recipe from and when I showed them they threw it in the bin.

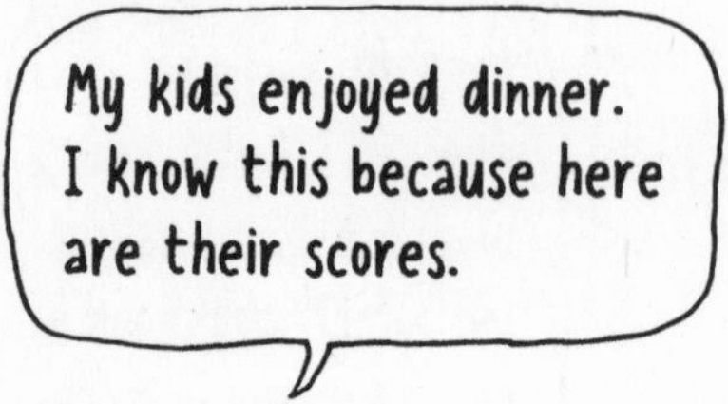
My kids enjoyed dinner. I know this because here are their scores.

My kids would have enjoyed their dinner. I know this, but they needed something to stick their pictures to the wall.

My kids enjoyed lunch. I know this because they've taped off the kitchen and declared it a crime scene.

My kids enjoyed dinner.
I know this because they just presented me with a plate of beans on toast they made & said "See, it's not difficult."

My kids enjoyed dinner. I know this because they've sent me to my room and told me to think very hard about what I'd done.

Weekends

The kids are having a bath. I know this because I can hear mum yelling "no!" & we currently have an attractive waterfall feature in the living room below.

I'm taking my kids to the hairdressers today. I know this because they are refusing to remove their bicycle helmets.

My kids are playing quietly upstairs. I know this because our neighbour's just been round to ask if he could have back the drill they borrowed.

I've finally managed to wash the kids' hair. I know this because they are currently in the kitchen spooning jam onto each other's heads.

My kids are playing nicely upstairs. I know this because the cat's just come into the front room in a hat and a pair of shorts.

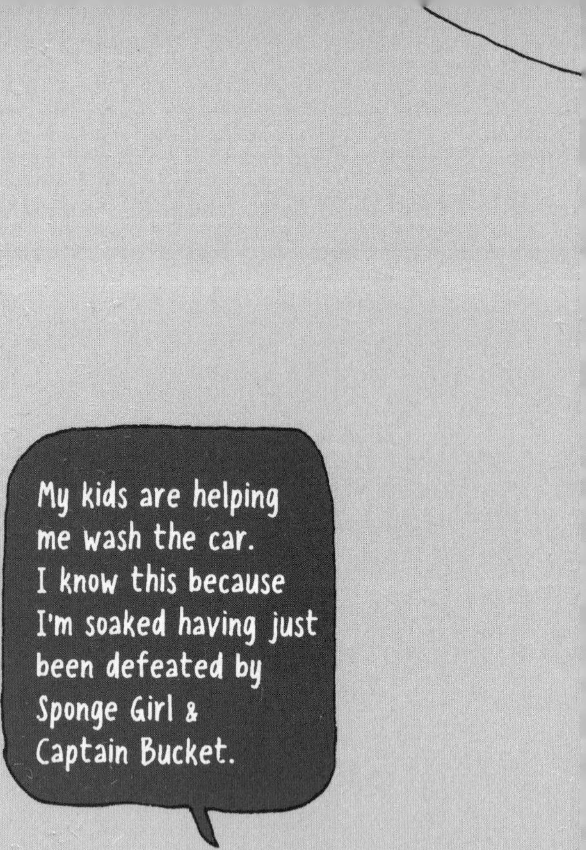
My kids are helping me wash the car. I know this because I'm soaked having just been defeated by Sponge Girl & Captain Bucket.

My kids are helping me unpack the shopping. I know this because the chocolate is no longer in the bag.

My kids are helping. I know this because they've tidied the biscuits up by eating them all.

My kids' room is tidy. I know this because after 2 weeks of negotiations with their union rep I tidied it.

My kids are helping. I know this because they're washing up and using my toothbrush as a scrubbing brush.

My kids helped me vacuum the front room. I know this because I can't find my keys, today's paper or the hamster.

My kids are helping me make lunch. I know this because today's lunch is strawberry ice cream, chocolate biscuits and marshmallows. And chocolate ice cream for pudding.

My kids have tidied all their toys off the floor. I know this because they're now all on the sofa.

My kids are helping me in the garden. I know this because someone from Mrs. Ripple's Party Hire has just delivered a bouncy castle.

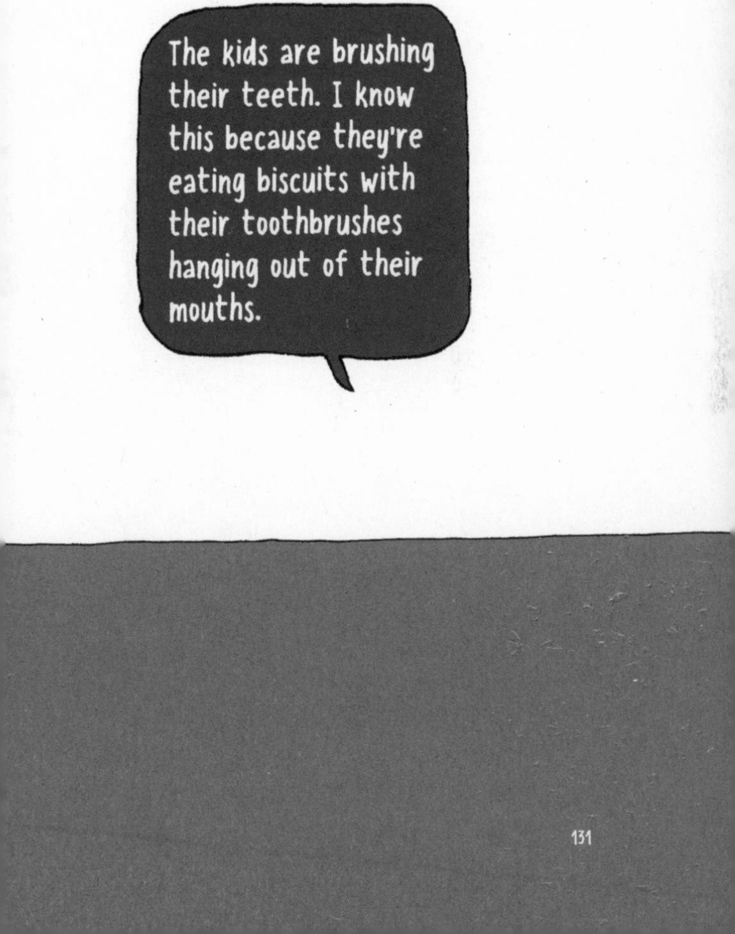
The kids are brushing their teeth. I know this because they're eating biscuits with their toothbrushes hanging out of their mouths.

My kids helped me weed the garden. I know this because I've just spent the last 3 hours replanting all the flowers.

My kids aren't bored.
I know this because
they are tweeting the
whole of Harry Potter
to me
           line

           by

                  line.